COLOR TEST PAGE

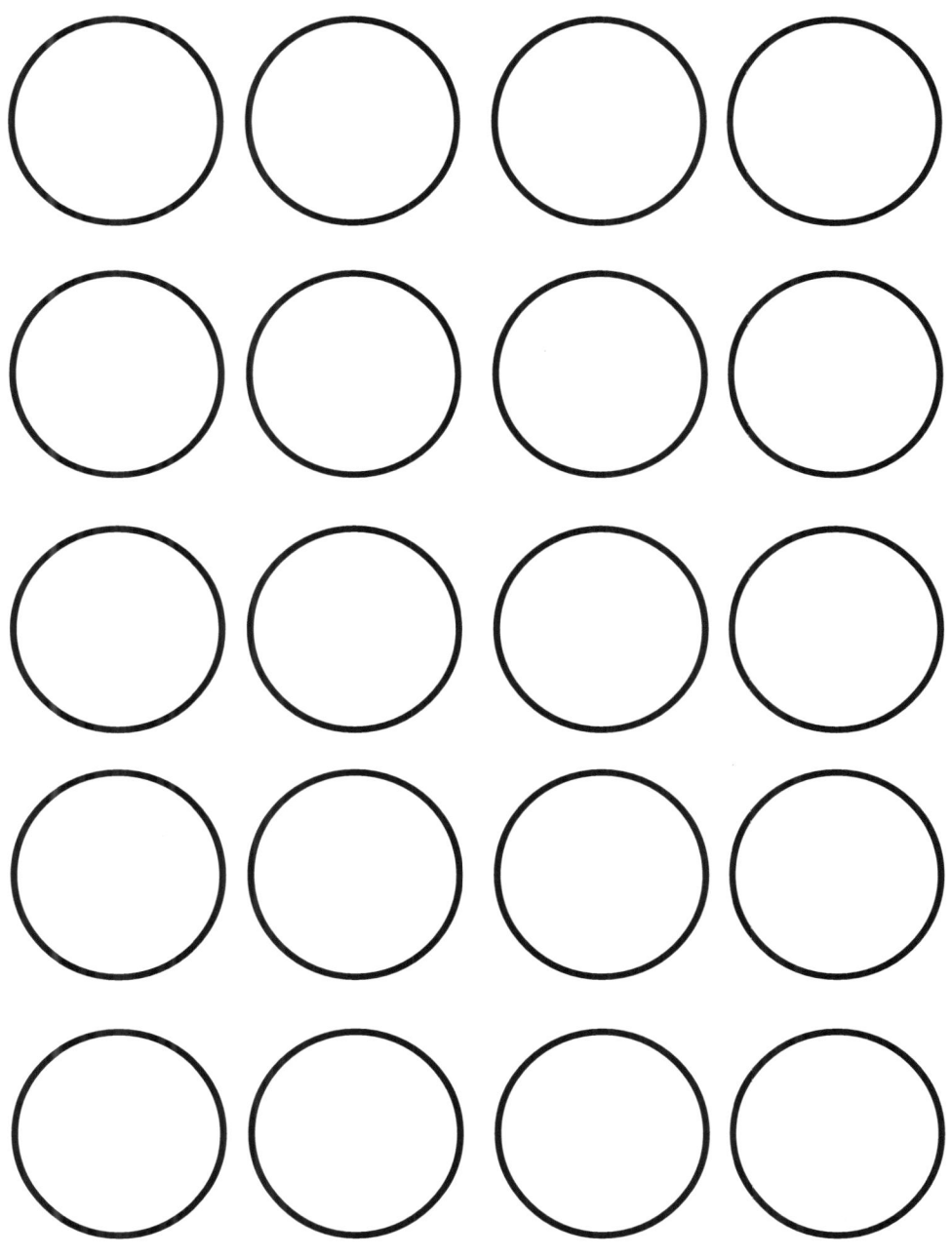

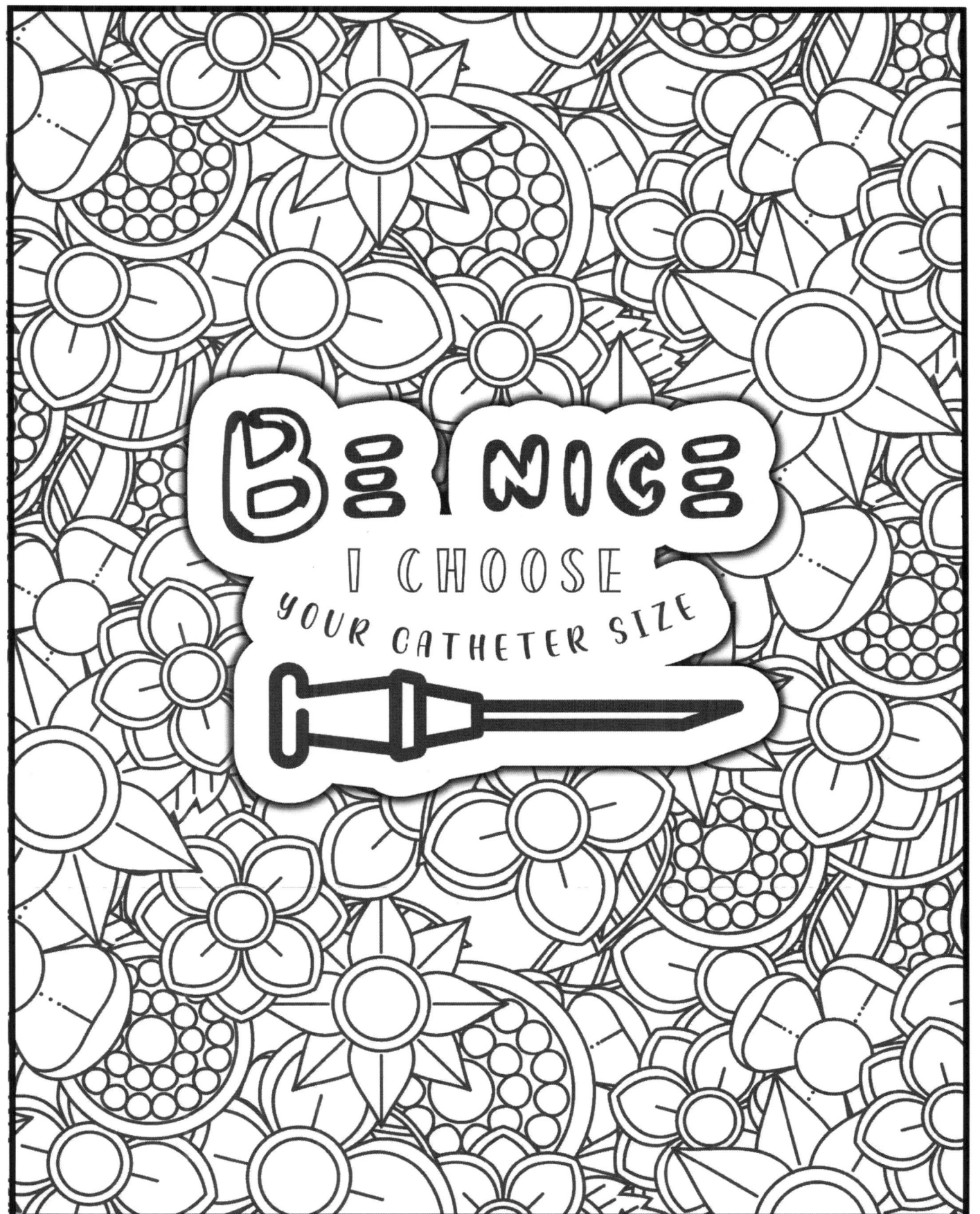

Yes I'M A NURSE NO I DON'T WANT to look at it

I see NAKED PEOPLE

Nursing is a walk in the PARK

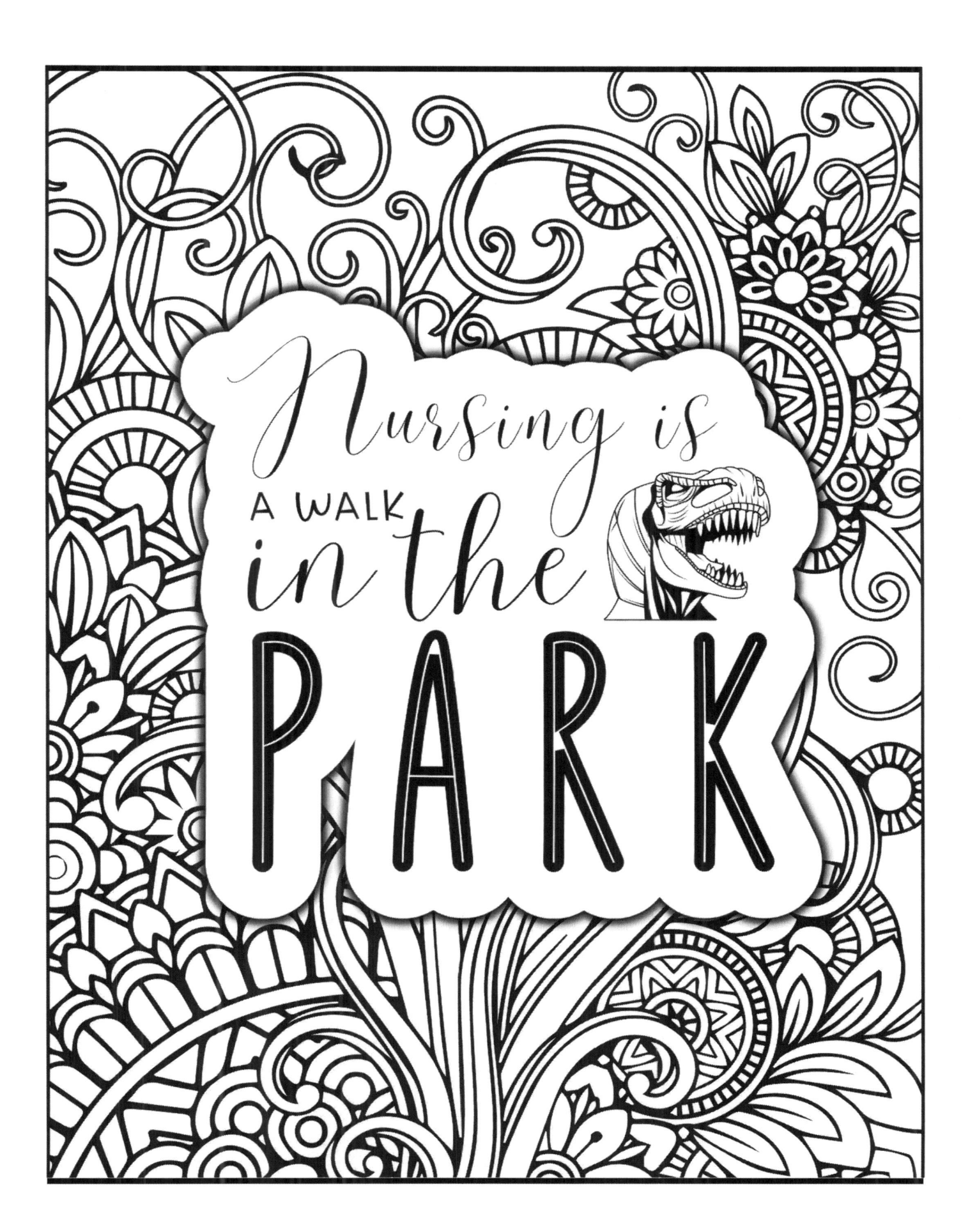

I can't cure **stupid** BUT I CAN SEDATE IT

A GOOD VEIN is what dreams ARE MADE OF

HAVE YOU TRIED **TURNING IT** OFF AND BACK ON AGAIN

— ADENOSINE

HELLO
my name is

HEY, NURSE

I don't have A NERVOUS system
___
I AM ONE

IF YOU'RE HAPPY AND YOU KNOW IT IT'S YOUR MEDS

NURSES: PATIENT PEOPLE

Ask me about AMA Forms

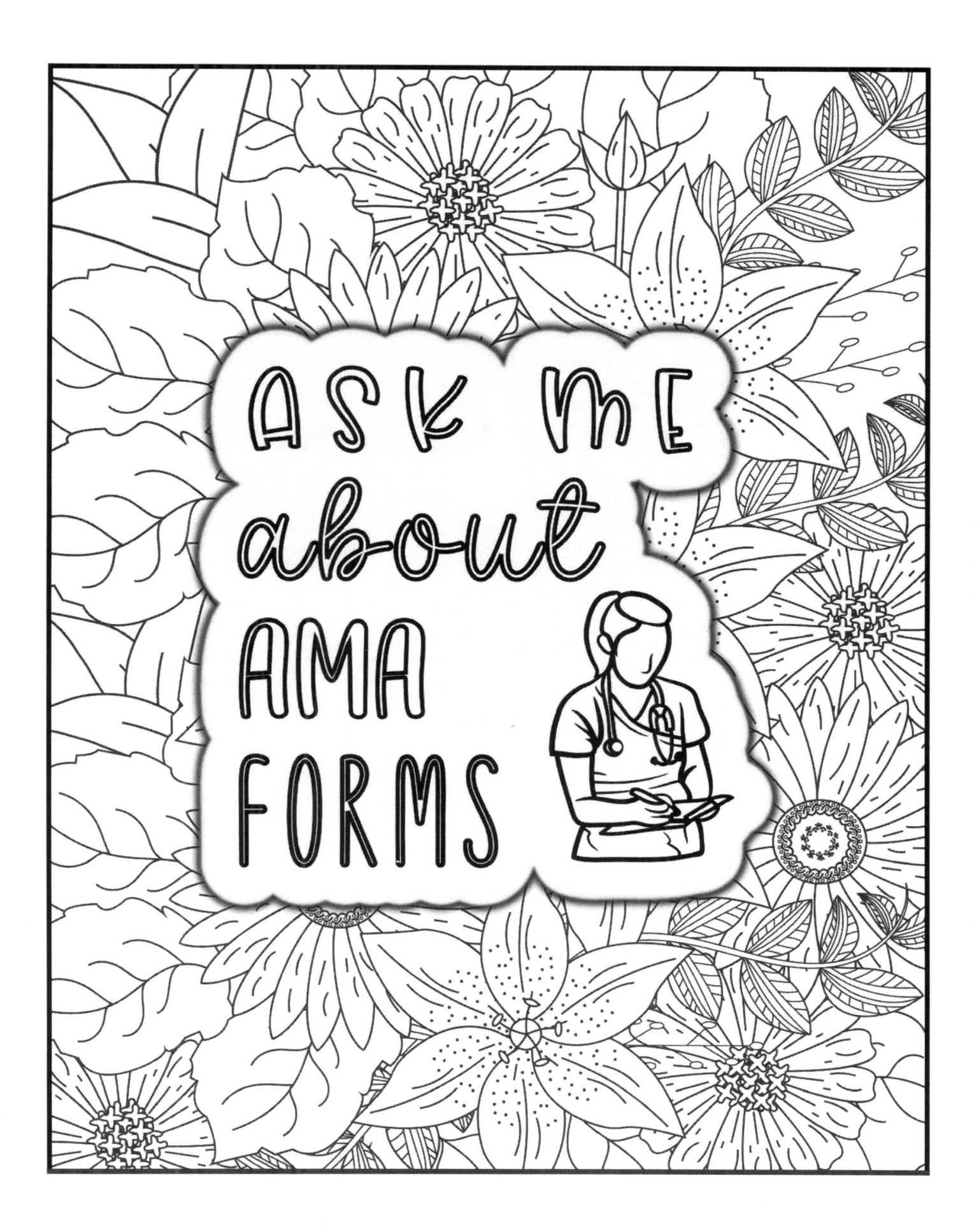

Don't you dare say THE Q WORD!

I WILL *Stab You*

WE BEND SO WE DON'T BREAK

Have you seen my BRAIN?

Remember this: Be kind to your mind

It's not in the pyxis, bin or fridge...

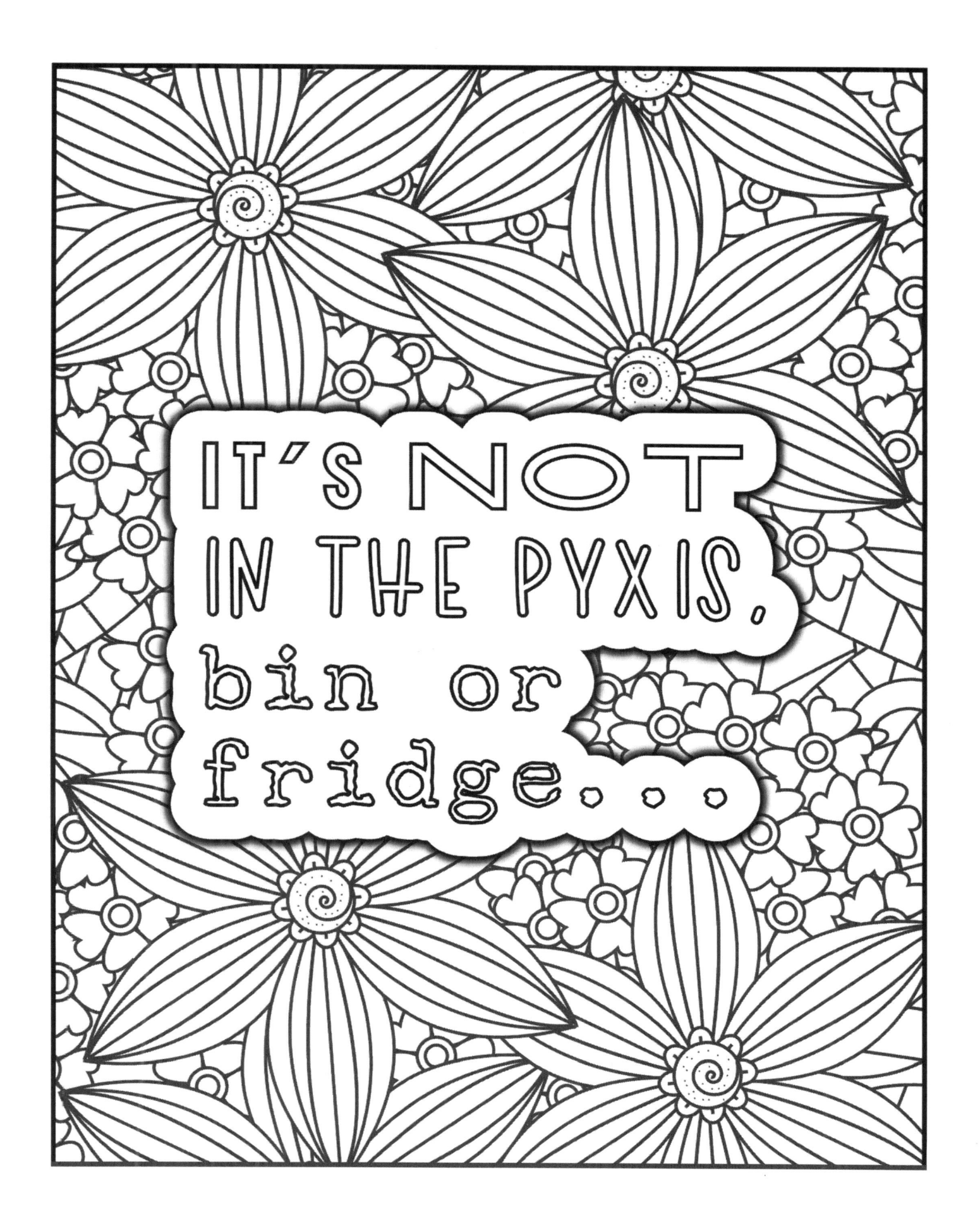

THAT SOUNDS LIKE A DSP

What happens in clinicals stays in clinicals

Coffee, SCRUBS and rubber GLOVES

ASK ME ABOUT *Southern Intubations*

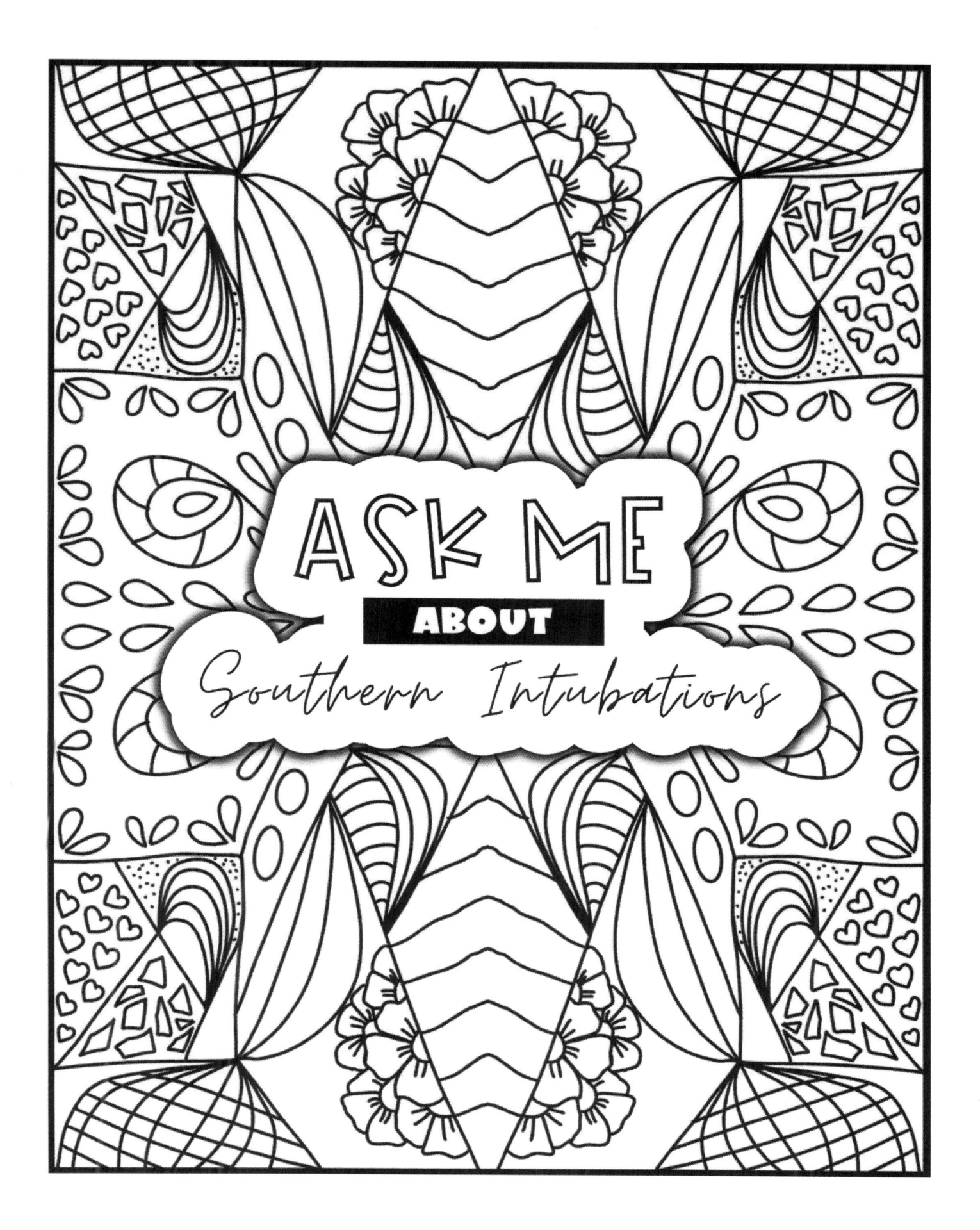

Do things at your own pace. Life's not a race.

NURSING SCHOOL survivor

I DIDN'T Quit today

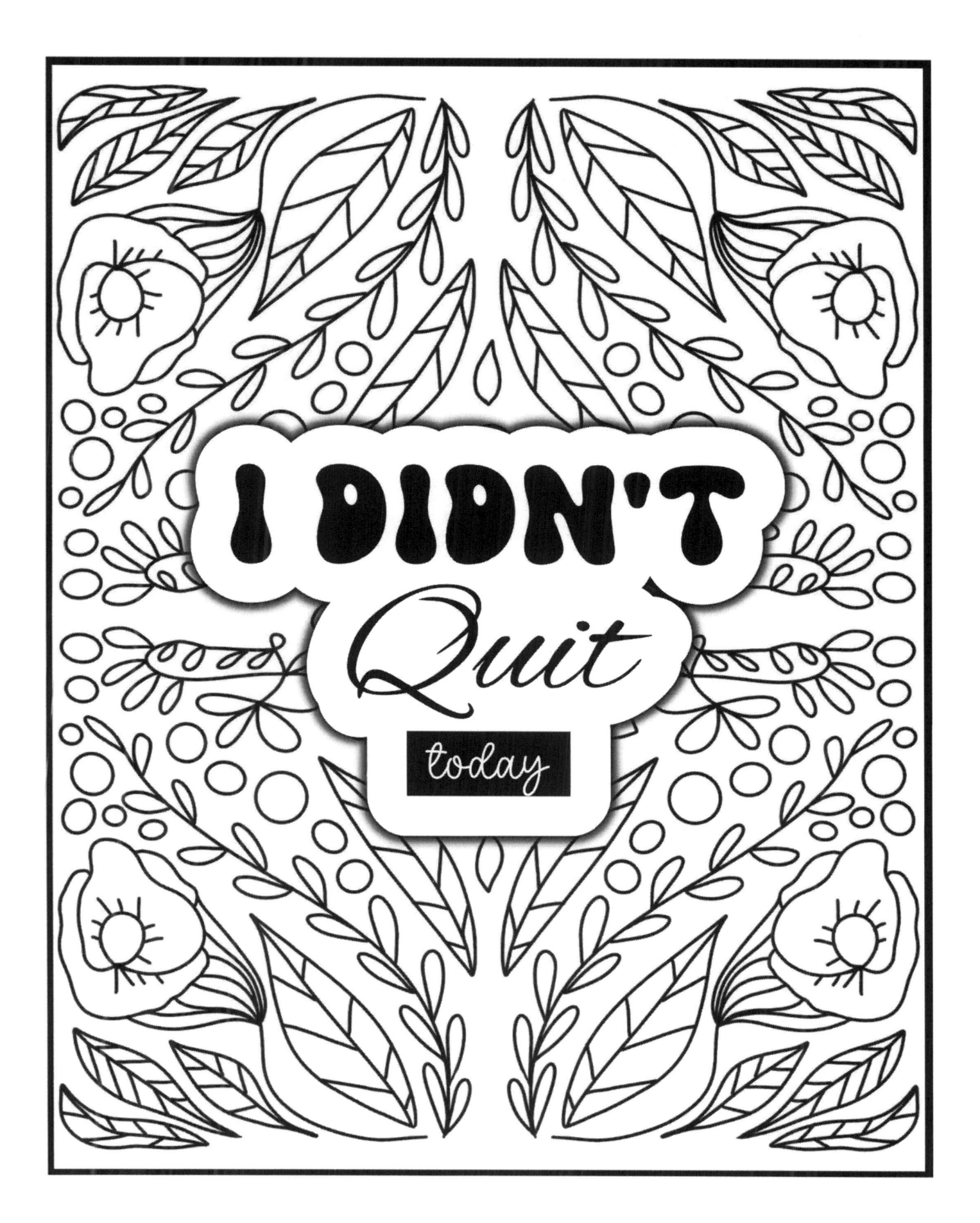

Instant NURSE just add COFFEE

Don't worry, I PRACTICED on a manequin ONCE

I STAB PEOPLE FOR A LIVING

I see MORE PRIVATE PARTS than a hooker

Educated DRUG DEALER

ONE MENTAL **BREAKDOWN** LATER...

Admit one

Hot Mess Express

Let's take a ride on the ATIVAN

SLEEP
nurse all night
ALL DAY

COPYRIGHT 2021 BY GERMAN STONE PRESS
CONTENT ILLUSTRATIONS LICENSED AND
SUBJECT TO COPYRIGHT. IN NO WAY IS IT LEGAL
TO REPRODUCE, DUPLICATE OR TRANSMIT ANY
PART OF THIS DOCUMENT BY EITHER ELECTRONIC
MEANS OR IN PRINTED FORMAT.

Made in the USA
Middletown, DE
18 February 2023